How to be a
Good
Mother-
in-Law

Bodleian Library
UNIVERSITY OF OXFORD

This edition first published in 2013 by the Bodleian Library
Broad Street
Oxford OX1 3BG
www.bodleianbookshop.co.uk
Reprinted in 2013

Abridged and edited from *Are You a Mother-in-Law? A Useful Guide for All in-Laws*, by Edgar and Diana Woods, first published in 1937 by Universal Publications Ltd., London.

ISBN: 978 1 85124 082 1

Cover design by Dot Little
Designed and typeset by JCS Publishing Services Ltd
Printed and bound in China by C&C Offset Printing Co. Ltd on 100gsm YuLong pure 1.3 paper

British Library Catalogue in Publishing Data
A CIP record of this publication is available from the British Library

PREFACE

THIS is, we believe, the first book that has ever been devoted exclusively to Mothers-in-law.

It deals with what is a burning subject without mincing matters. Thus, every mother-in-law and everybody who has a mother-in-law will want to read it.

No one person is likely to agree with every word that is written; nevertheless, most of our readers will admit that the matter has been set out in a manner that is long overdue.

CONTENTS

I

A SEARCHLIGHT ON MOTHERS-IN-LAW

THERE are two main types of mothers-in-law, those you would not suspect as holding this particular office, and those who leave no doubt in your mind about it.

The first are deserving of much sympathy, because their position is made difficult by the second. The second are, of course, those who provide the material which humorists work up into jokes.

Unfortunately, one does not have to be remarkably smart to create jokes about mothers-in-law, because some mothers-in-law unconsciously provide all the material necessary for the purpose.

The question will arise in anybody's mind as to why the term *mother-in-law* has a flavour of opprobrium which is entirely absent from the parallel relationship of *father-in-law*. Is it because the office of father-in-law is an easier one to fill than that of mother-in-law? The answer is *no*, because they are practically the same. Is it because the father-in-law does not face up to the situation like a man, but leaves all the dirty work to be done by the mother-in-law? Here again the answer is *no*. Then what can be the underlying reason for attaching opprobrium to the term *mother-in-law* and viewing the parallel term *father-in-law* in an entirely dispassionate light? We think the answer lies in the fact that women concern themselves more than men do with the *home*, and it is very much with home matters that mothers-in-law can interfere and get themselves a bad name.

It would not surprise us if, in this last sentence we have not touched the very root of the matter and put on record for the first time the real reason why so many mothers-in-law make themselves unpopular. *They interfere with the home matters of their married sons and daughters.*

This brings us to the question, *Why do they make themselves a nuisance by interfering?* Of course, there is a variety of reasons, but the chief are:—

(a) They cannot realise that their child has grown up and is living a life of its own. They have always been in the habit of ordering it about and they continue to do so.

(b) They cannot understand that the child views life from a more modern angle than they do; therefore when it does a thing in a different way from their method of doing it, they conclude the method is wrong and immediately set about putting things right.

(c) They don't consider that their son or daughter has a good enough partner and they itch to let the partner know their opinion.

Now, if you are a mother-in-law and want a little sound advice, never interfere with your married children, their homes and their possessions. If you do you will soon find that you are not wanted. If your opinion is sought, give it; but be circumspect how you give it. If your opinion is not sought, don't volunteer it just because you feel you ought. Keep to these simple rules and you will be more than a welcome visitor to the new home.

II

THE first duty of a mother-in-law arises before she actually is a mother-in-law. It arises, in fact, at the time when her son or daughter begins to show a real preference for somebody.

A lot will depend on how the mother-in-law-to-be treats that *somebody* from the start.

If she asserts her authority unduly, if she is unreasonable, or if she "sniffs" at the newcomer, the latter will be quick to notice it and will never forgive her. And later on, when the newcomer has become an accomplished fact, he or she will not have much cause for being sympathetic towards the mother-in-law.

He or she will just about tolerate the latter, or do even less than that.

Therefore, first impressions are very important, and any sensible woman with a thought for the future will do her very utmost to be nice to any possible *in-law* that may come along.

Of course, nobody is going to contend that the office of mother-in-law is as simple as A B C. It certainly calls for tact. For, while it is folly to be austere and unreasonable, it is not wise to be over-nice, especially when the future *in-law* happens to be of the male sex. "Hallo," the Timid young may say to himself, "this is a match-making mother; I'm off." And that will be the end of that.

Accordingly, the future mother-in-law must strike a happy mean between the two extremes, with perhaps a bias on the pleasant side.

In many ways, the future mother-in-law has exceptional opportunities for endearing herself to the newcomer of the family. Her very position affords her unlimited scope in that matter.

Naturally, it is not a pleasant thing for someone to come along and deprive you of your son or daughter; but mothers-in-law have no reason for complaining. They permitted exactly the same thing to happen in their own case years ago.

Then, of course, there is the question of family pride. Nobody thinks more than a mother-in-law does that blood is thicker than water, with the result that, in her heart, she never feels that the person who her son or daughter intends to marry is good enough for her son or daughter.

There is no earthly reason why she should not think these things if she wants to. But there is every reason why she should keep such thoughts to herself.

A catty remark, casually dropped; a haughty look, a pursing of the lips—these and a dozen other danger signals coming from a prospective mother-in-law will speak volumes to the one who has come a-courting and they will not be easily forgotten.

Not only should a prospective mother-in-law keep these thoughts about the newcomer not being good enough to herself; but she should keep them from her son or daughter, unless there is some abundantly good reason for stopping the marriage altogether.

What, for instance, will be the frame of mind of, say, a daughter who brings home her young man whom she adores and, rightly enough, thinks is perfection; when her mother sniffs and says, "Well, I should have thought you could have got something better than that."

It is enough to make the daughter see red, and she will never forgive her mother. Certainly it will put up a barrier between the two which will never be entirely swept away.

Now let us turn to a slightly different aspect of the whole situation. Everybody knows that the girl's people and the man's people seldom mix well. It happens in nine cases out of ten that neither family has much time for the other.

This is a great pity, because what it means is that the young couple will be very lucky if they are able to steer clear of quarrels between themselves on the subject. In fact, many married people will tell you that their first tiff was about "his people" or "her people."

The question thus arises, "Why is it that the two sides of the family are so often at loggerheads?"

It all happens like this: The prospective mother-in-law may be openly hostile to the person her son or daughter intends to marry and, then, all their relations will be promptly classed in the same boat. Or she may be averse to showing definite hostility to the person her son or daughter proposes to marry, yet the hostility is still there and she must fix it somewhere. Who more fitting to be the recipients of her sneers than the person's family? Thus "his people" or "her people" become the butt of her feelings and she goes all out to belittle them.

Of course, when she sets the pace and the ball starts rolling, it is not difficult for her to enlist the sympathies of those around her.

Mind you, we have not forgotten that there is an opposite number in the shape of a mother-in-law on the other side of the family, who may be acting in exactly the same way. Thus, the average marriage can mean two hostile camps, under the generalship of two very able mothers-in-law.

In concluding this section, we offer these few "don'ts" to prospective mothers-in-law.

Don't feel aggrieved because your son or daughter has found somebody he or she likes. You did the same thing once.

Don't think that it was all right in your case, but wrong in his or hers.

Don't try to stop the match, unless you have more than a good reason. Disparity in ages may be a good reason; but snobbishness is not.

Don't think that *marrying well*, as it is vulgarly called in fashionable circles, must necessarily lead to happiness. It often misses the mark.

Don't fail to look for the newcomer's good

qualities and to shut your eyes to his or her faults, as long as they do not loom too large.

Don't make him or her feel uncomfortable, when in your presence, by putting on an air of superiority.

Do, however, welcome him or her as nicely and affectionately as you would a child of your own. Give the *somebody* to understand that you are entrusting your child to his or her care and that you expect the said *somebody* to watch over its happiness in the future as you have done in the past.

III

RECENTLY, a letter was printed in one of the
morning papers which was written by a girl
who was complaining about the woman who
might become her mother-in-law.

The burden of the complaint was that the
future mother-in-law refused to meet the girl
and acknowledge her as the son's possible
bride.

Obviously, you may think, the mother-
in-law had some good reason for refusing
to meet the girl and acknowledging her. She
knew the girl was too young or too old, or too
something.

The letter to which we have referred clearly stated that the mother-in-law elect had never seen the girl, did not know her and did not want to. Thus, there was no question of the mother-in-law thinking that the girl was more unsuitable than any other girl for her son.

In fact, it is more than probable that, had the girl been an angel descended from Heaven, she would have been accorded exactly the same treatment. In any case, she would have been snubbed.

This gives rise to the question, *Why should the prospective mother-in-law want to snub the girl?*

Many mothers-in-law reason to themselves in this manner: "If I acknowledge the girl, it will help things on and I don't want to help things on, because the easier it is for my son the quicker he will get married and, of course, I don't want him to get married, seeing that I shall lose him when he is married."

Mark you, there is no consideration for the son's feelings in any of this, which is rather curious, nor for those of the girl, which is not curious. Such a mother-in-law is thinking of nobody but herself.

For the benefit of all concerned, we should like to address the following words to every mother-in-law who thinks it clever to refuse to meet her son's girl. (Of course, what we say is equally applicable when the position is reversed and it is a daughter's young man who is shunned.)

Dear Madam,

You know full well that love is a curious thing which cannot be explained or fully accounted for. Also, you probably know that it cannot be conjured up at will nor thrust aside voluntarily. In fact, it is something inexplicable.

Now you are daring to trifle with this inexplicable force, owing to some selfish motives of your own. Don't you understand that if you drive this girl away from your son, you may be denying him the greatest happiness which life can bring him?

"Ah," you probably say, "let him wait." Yes, but he may wait to please you and he may marry some other girl in ten or fifteen years' time. And all the remainder of his days there may be the picture of this girl, whom you are proposing to drive away, torturing his imagination. This girl may be *the* one for him. You don't know if it is or it is not, yet you are quite satisfied to risk damaging the remainder of his life for your own selfish ends.

Now, suppose you try your hardest to drive away the girl and fail to succeed. Your son, in fact, marries her. What is the position?

Do you straightway haul down the flag and say, "Now we will be friends," because, if you do, the girl may not see things in your light. She may tell you, without any beating about the bush, that she does not need your friendship, and she will be perfectly within her rights if she does. You have been uncouth to her and it is now her turn to play the trump card.

Perhaps, in your conceit, you may think that the moment you are ready to be friends the girl will embrace your advances. Don't be too sure of that. There is such a thing as pride, and the girl may have her share of it.

If the girl is ready to say "Let bygones be bygones," she will only say it for one reason, and that reason is because she knows it will be a decent thing to do for her husband's sake. It will not be prompted by any affection for you.

"Well," you may say, as a last resort, "if my son marries that girl, I never want to know her." Many mothers-in-law have said exactly these words; some of them have found to their cost, very quickly, that they would have been better left unsaid; others have taken longer to find out their folly; but few have gained any advantage by uttering them.

Just note what the words mean. They mean that, if you do not want to know the girl, you will see very little of your son henceforth. Do you want that?

"Oh, but he will come to see me by himself." Is it likely that he will visit you more than once in a while if he cannot bring his wife? And when there are grandchildren, do you think the girl will let you see them? It is not very likely.

But the worst side of the picture, as it concerns you, portrays the situation in twenty or more years hence. You will be an old lady; your son and daughter-in-law will be middle-aged. More than likely, some of your friends will have gone and loneliness will be your portion. It is then that sons and daughters-in-law can repay the kindnesses that were showered on them in their youth. Will your daughter-in-law be in your debt? If she comes and takes pity on you it will be because she is a better woman than ever you were.

Thus, taken all in all, you are following an insane course if you are in any way harsh towards your prospective daughter-in-law or son-in-law. To refuse to meet them or allow them to visit your home is making things difficult for them now and for you in years to come.

First impressions count a great deal, and if you act in such a way that the prospective *in-law* gets a bad impression of you, then you are only making a rod for your own back.

IV

WAIT!

WHY is it that, when a son wants to marry, his mother, who is a potential mother-in-law, tells him, in nine cases out of ten, to wait?

It does not matter whether the son is twenty, thirty or forty, his mother still says *wait*.

Of course, if the son is eighteen and his mother says *wait*, one concludes that she is prompted by beneficial motives towards the son; but if she still says the same thing when he is twenty-eight or thirty-eight, it becomes rather doubtful whether she has his good at heart as much as she pretends.

Naturally, it is not the most satisfactory thing in the world for a mother to have a son, to bring him up, to watch over his interests, his pleasures and troubles, and then to "lose" him.

But we have to face facts as they are, and these are the facts which constitute the normal development of existence. It is no more use kicking against them than trying to turn night into day.

But mothers do kick against them and, in doing so, make themselves abominably unpopular.

Of course, a mother says *wait*, in the hope of putting off what to her is the evil day. It may succeed and it may not.

If it does not succeed, it means that the son has ignored his mother, that she has lowered herself in his eyes and that she has lost popularity.

If it does succeed, she has gained a little satisfaction for herself, and made two people unhappy. Probably her satisfaction is only temporary because the whole question is likely to arise again, and perhaps again.

Well, is it worth it? Does the mother derive any real advantage by being awkward? There is only one answer, and that is *No*.

What are the conditions which arise through her habit of saying *wait*? First of all, a son who anticipates this fiat will most likely resort to a subterfuge. He will tell his mother nothing until the whole business is a *fait accompli* and then he will announce the fact.

This puts the mother in an awkward position, and it may give her a nasty shock. Does she relish that? Also, it gives the girl, who now becomes the wife, a very real feeling that her newly-made mother-in-law is an unpleasant person—a trouble-maker in fact. Is that desirable?

But suppose the mother has such a hold over her son that he does *wait*. The son, then, has to go and tell the girl his mother has frightened him into waiting. What the girl will think of him need not be discussed. What would any girl think under the circumstances?

So, look at it as you will, this habit which mothers have of trying to postpone the wedding of their sons is a dangerous one. It seldom does any good and usually it does harm.

It harms the mother in her capacity of mother-in-law, since it puts her on bad terms from the start, with the two young people, and it harms the son and daughter-in-law because it upsets all their plans and all the castles in the air that they have built.

Of course, there are times when it is advisable to wait, but they are not a hundredth part as numerous as mothers try to make out.

A young man of our acquaintance, who was not married, and is never likely to be, told us, "ever since I was eighteen my mother has told me that I should get married in ten years' time."

V

CAUSING TROUBLE

FOR many years, we have studied mothers-in-law as some people study medicine and others become absorbed in stamp-collecting. We have listened to them, taken notes of their conversations and tried to humour their sometimes unreasonable wants. We have done the same thing with fathers-in-law and found them far less interesting, since they are not anything like so assertive in the role which their children force on them.

Now, we have only once or twice heard a father-in-law talk disparagingly to his son about wives; but on the other hand we have grown to look upon mothers-in-law telling their daughters about the villainies of husbands as a stable article of conversation.

Thus the question arises, "What fun can a mother-in-law get out of telling her daughter that husbands are all alike, or that none of them are any good?" Of course, if only one here and there made the assertion, the matter could be ignored; but of the trouble-making kind of mother-in-law, practically all indulge in spreading the libel.

Only the other day, we met a man whom we always felt was a very decent husband, and who probably considered that nothing but the best was good enough for his wife. We could easily sense that he was not himself and after a while the fact came out by accident that he had had a quarrel with his wife.

Seeing that the secret was revealed, he took us into his confidence and told us all about the quarrel. The story is easily recounted. A day or two before, while he was at the office, his mother-in-law had been round to the house and had thrashed out her favourite topic that men were all alike and that none of them were any good.

The wife had listened to the tirade and, for some reason, had given it credence, probably because the words had come from her own mother.

It so happened that on that night, the man was detained at the office and reached home very late. Now, one of the pieces of advice vouchsafed by the mother-in-law was, *Never believe a man when he comes home late and says he has been detained at the office. You know straight away that he has been drinking with his worthless friends.*

The wife, who was at heart a mild creature, waited somewhat impatiently for her husband's return and, when he did get in, listened to the story that he had been kept late at the office. This was too much for her to swallow, coming so soon after her mother's words of wisdom, and she burst into tears.

The husband was dumbfounded and pressed to know what the scene was all about.

After some coaxing the wife, more in sorrow than in anger, asked him pleadingly why he had told her a lie about being kept at the office when she knew he had been drinking with friends.

Why should she think such unfounded things? The husband wanted to know, and then, piece by piece, the mother-in-law's tirade was unfolded.

You may ask, then how did the quarrel occur between the husband and wife? Well, that arose over the things the husband said about his mother-in-law. All he maintained was probably true; but the wife, owing to misplaced loyalty to her mother, abused him for saying them.

Unfortunately, this little tragedy which we have recounted is by no means an isolated one and there are mothers-in-law all up and down the country who cause trouble in exactly the same way.

Here are some things that you should not say to your daughter, if you are a mother-in-law and wish her to remain happy:—

(a) It is a mistake to trust any man.

(b) A husband is no good if he does not get up in the morning and make his wife a cup of tea.

(c) Don't always be in when your husband arrives home. Let him know what it is like to be at home by himself.

(d) Don't fuss round your husband. Make him fuss round you.

(e) Don't put up with his relations.

In fact, don't put ideas into your daughter's head that she should rule her husband. In a proper partnership, neither of the two wants any show of superiority over the other.

VI

WHY is it that mothers-in-law think so much of their own dignity? Dignity may be all very well in its proper place, but when it does not suit the occasion, it is either funny or aggravating.

Far too many mothers-in-law have an idea that dignity gives them an importance which would be lacking otherwise. Accordingly they assume this form of play-acting when the occasion seems to demand it.

Obviously, this dignity is meant to impress those of the younger generation who have married or are about to marry their sons and daughters. But does it? These young people either go away vowing vengeance or they burst into roars of laughter, round the corner.

It seems remarkable that a mother-in-law would act in this way to those who have entered her family by way of the altar. But this behaviour does occur, nevertheless.

How often have you seen a woman as lively as a cricket until her daughter-in-law entered the room, and then change her whole tone and become as unapproachable as a judge? We are sad to say that we have noticed it on more than one occasion.

Apparently, the idea is to show the daughter-in-law, or it may be a son-in-law, that she or he and the mother are as far apart as the poles; that one is at the top of everything and the other at the bottom.

Of course, we are not going to say that there are no mothers-in-law who treat their daughters-in-law in a kindly way. But too many fall into this unfortunate trap.

Now, here is a case in point. We had always imagined that a certain woman of

our acquaintance was too high-minded to play the usual run of mothers-in-law, and we were round at her house the other day. The conversation turned to her married son, and we idly put the usual question, "How is he and Mary getting on?" The woman immediately changed her whole manner. "That daughter-in-law of mine," she said, "is more than I can understand. Why, last Monday she was here, and her flippancy was disgraceful. Do you know, she started to tell me that, the day before, she had met a girl friend of hers who lived at Earl's Court and she said she told the girl that her mother-in-law lived at Earl's Court as well. Now, what do you think of that?"

From the way the words were repeated, we knew that we were supposed to look shocked, so we obliged by looking shocked; though we had not the faintest idea as to what particular thing or word was to blame, and we would not mind hazarding a guess that the reader is equally in the dark.

After a suitable pause, we said, "Yes—well—and what did you say?" hoping in this way to plumb the depths of Mary's cardinal sin. And here is our friend's answer, uttered in dramatic, measured tones: "I looked at Mary straight in the eye," she began, "and I said to her, 'Mary, please understand that, in the future, you don't use the words *mother-in-law*. In speaking to friends, you say *Fred's mother*, and in business conversations you say, *My husband's mother*.'"

"And what did Mary say to that?" we enquired. "Nothing," came the answer, which seemed to suggest that Mary was squashed. That evening we thought a lot about Mary, wondering whether she did say anything, but waited until after. We rather think we know the answer. Before leaving the story, it might be illuminating to turn back to the beginning and note how this mother-in-law first spoke of Mary. Should it not have been *Fred's wife* or *My son's wife*, as the circumstances required?

This perfectly true story illustrates the unnatural dignity which mothers-in-law assume on far too many occasions. Of course, they do not necessarily adopt the same preposterous method of displaying it, but they display it all the same.

VII

VISITING A MARRIED DAUGHTER

THE following is an open letter which might reasonably be sent to any mothers-in-law on the eve of a visit they are paying to their daughters:—

Dear Madam,

To-morrow you are going to set out for a week's stay with Edith and her husband, and everybody trusts you will have an excellent time. Edith and Tom are looking forward to your arrival and it is to be hoped that nothing will happen that will make them look forward to your departure.

They know that mothers-in-law have not the best of names; but they do not consider you to be true to type and they are certainly not going to look for trouble. So, you see, the stage is set for an enjoyable week and it is to be hoped that nothing will arise to spoil it.

As you have never before played the part of a mother-in-law for a whole seven days, perhaps a few words coming from us will not be amiss.

In the first place, it might be well to point out that Edith and Tom are rather proud of their little home. Therefore, as soon as you arrive, do not begin to litter up the place with your personal effects. They want you to feel comfortable, it is true; but if you throw your coat over the sofa-back, put your hat on the piano-top, keep the medicine bottle, which you have to uncork three times a day, on the mantelpiece, spread the necessaries of knitting on the chairs, and throw the newspapers on the floor when you have failed to do the crossword puzzles, then the trouble will begin.

Edith likes the place to be nice and tidy when Tom comes home tired at night, and if she has to run round and do a sort of miniature spring clean when he is expected, it will not lighten her duties, which are already heavy enough.

Then, when Tom does come home and you all sit down to the evening meal, let Tom get a word in edgeways. You see, he has had no opportunities for talking with Edith about his day and there are, naturally, things he wants to tell her. On the other hand, you will have been with her most of the day and you can have your little chats then.

Above all, the thing you must not do is to turn the conversation on to people you and Edith know, but Tom does not. You may think it important to discuss the fittings on the perambulator owned by the new baby belonging to the girl who once spoke to Edith when there was a fire in your aunt's coal shed. And Edith may appear to be interested, but it will be jolly hard for Tom to stand much of it. Thus, if you happen to pick the subjects for discussion, let them be of a nature that even Tom may discourse on intelligently.

Of course, while it is wrong for you to monopolise the conversation, it is equally or even more distressing if you fail to do your share of the speaking. There is a kind of mother-in-law who sits down very primly, who eats with precision, and who refuses to say more than *Yes* or *No*. If you do that, Edith and Tom will begin to exchange glances, and both will become very uncomfortable.

Edith, naturally, has had very little experience in running a home and you have had lots. Therefore, it goes without saying that there are a good many things you can teach her. It will only be mother-like if you give her the benefit of your experience; but be very careful how you do it.

The way you should *not* do it is as follows: We will suppose that dinner commences. A plate of soup is set before you and you immediately exclaim, "What a pity the soup is cold! Now, if you would only do so and so, it would come to the table piping hot." Then the joint is brought on and you eye it wistfully. "Ah!" you say, "if you don't want one end to be cooked to cinders and the other end to be absolutely raw, you should have a slower oven." Finally, a rice pudding is served and, having taken just one mouthful, you volunteer the information that a rice pudding is not worth eating unless it is made according to your own pet way.

If you run through the various items on the menu in this manner, you will be merely patting yourself on the back at Edith's expense. Just remember that Tom probably thinks that his little wife has done marvellously for the time she has been managing a home, and he is very proud of her. Good luck to him, we say. So, when you wax eloquently on the way to keep soup hot or the way to make creamy rice puddings, you are merely asking him to shout from the house tops that he prefers cold soup to mothers-in-law. And Edith, in her heart of hearts, will say "Hear, hear."

It will be quite easy to give Edith all the hundred and one hints which will help her to become efficient, if you go about it in the right way and do it at the right time. The right time will be when she and you are alone together and when she is not preoccupied with the butcher and the baker.

Of course, if the house is a servantless one and Edith has forgotten to put out salt and pepper, don't tell Tom to go and get them with some such remark as, "Edith has been working all day and is tired." For one thing, Tom will resent taking orders from anybody, and, for another, it may be that Tom did something in the nature of work while he was at business. And, if you ostentatiously offer to go and get the salt and pepper yourself, you are putting Tom in an awkward position, should you be allowed to go. Naturally, the proper course is for you to refrain from interfering and to let the salt and pepper find its way to the table as best it can.

It may be that Tom is one of those men who are not very useful in the home, and it may be that he is not particularly thoughtful. He may remark on the absence of the salt and pepper and expect Edith to jump up and fetch it. Well, that may make your blood boil. Granted that it is not the best way for a man to act towards his wife, but if your blood boils, just let it go on boiling. If you tell him half of what you would like to, you will make an awful mess of things and if you say nothing but look daggers, it will be just as fatal. For one thing, don't forget that Edith may belong to the type of women who hate to see a man doing domestic services, holding the opinion that it is only tame kittens who do. Anyway, your job is to sit tight and do absolutely nothing.

From all this, you may begin to think that your visit is going to be a week of minding your p's and q's. No, it need not be, if you will only act reasonably. As long as you don't try to put everybody and everything right, things should go along nicely and comfortably. For instance, do not march into the drawing-room and, having inspected it, say, "What a nice room, but —" Anybody can criticise anything, and a "but" coming from a mother-in-law is the red rag to a bull. Therefore, don't say that the piano would be better in the other corner, and when you spot a framed photograph on the wall, of a person whom you know must be Tom's father, don't say, "Who's that man?" sniffing suitably as you ask the question.

Tom, if he is the right sort, will want you to have a royal time while you are under his roof. Moreover, he will hope that Edith will enjoy your stay. If he gives you *carte blanche* to do what you like while your visit lasts, do not take him too literally. We once knew a newly-married couple who made some such expression to the wife's mother, and within an hour she announced that she had invited a doddering old Mrs. Brown to dinner on Tuesday, the ugly Misses Jones to play cards on Wednesday, and other friends, who had spent some time in the Ark, on subsequent evenings. Now that was taking the offer too literally; in fact it was

a piece of impudence on the part of the wife's mother, even though she had had *carte blanche* to do as she liked.

If you think that some of your friends who happen to live near Edith and not near you might reasonably be invited during your stay, then consult Edith quietly on the matter. It may be that she would rather not be forced into knowing them, or she may be prepared to ask them to come to tea and not dinner. In fact, she may be prepared to have them, if she can get them out of the way before Tom comes home. Anyway, don't electrify the young things with a *fait accompli*, or it will look as though you intend to take charge of the establishment.

Then there is just one more thing we want to touch on before bringing this letter to a close. It is this: During your stay, it may be that you and Edith will plan to go out somewhere together. Perhaps it will be to the theatre, the "pictures," a shopping expedition or one of a dozen other diversions. Well, if something of this kind is arranged, let your daughter make the plans and see to it that you fall in with them.

She may be very anxious to reach home before Tom does, or she may have other reasons for wanting to be back by a certain time. She may not feel disposed to explain her reasons to you; but if she tells you that she wishes to get home first, don't pooh-pooh the idea. Above all, don't tell her that it will do Tom good to reach home and find you out. Many mothers-in-law have said exactly that and they are downright mischief-makers.

Having said our say, we will close with the hope that your visit will be enjoyable in every way to all concerned.

VIII

ABOUT MARRIED SONS

MANY mothers feel that a load has been taken off their minds when one of their daughters marries; but few mothers view it as anything but a loss when a son shoulders the responsibilities of matrimony.

Of course, it is perfectly unreasonable that they should hold such views and make such unfortunate differentiations between sons and daughters; but there it is, such feelings do tend to come to the surface.

Subconsciously, the mother-in-law looks upon her son's wife as a poor specimen of womanhood; or perhaps she holds this view more blatantly than subconsciously. You see, the son chose the girl without consulting the mother, and, in the nature of things, he must have been wrong.

Some mothers-in-law have a way of putting two and two together, and when they do so the result often comes to five and, maybe, six. Translated into plain English, this means that after the son has been married a short while, his mother begins to detect things.

She is fairly anxious to find a weak spot somewhere and she hunts around to seek out a red light burning brightly; and, of course, a red light is found, right enough.

The red light may take one of a hundred forms. Usually it has something to do with Harry's health. He may have a cough. If so, the cough has nothing to do with smoking too many cigarettes, nor with coming out of a hot dance-room into the freezing night air, nor even with breathing the foul air of the Tube trains. Oh, dear no! It's the way Mary neglects him. "It's her fault and she doesn't look after him as she should."

Of course, if Harry's health is so unreasonable that it absolutely refuses to give his mother the chance she wants, then something else must provide the necessary bone of contention. A favourite theme, then, will prove to be what we will call his "happiness," and the argument in all such cases will go something like this: "Poor Harry! I'm as certain as anything that he isn't happy, and however could he be with such a wife? Harry, you know, was always such an intelligent boy and so bright, and, of course, Mary hasn't two ideas in her head."

So, you see, if Harry has a cough, it is put down to the fact that Mary does not see that the bedclothes are aired; if he has indigestion it is due to her bad cooking; if he has business worries at the office, she is said to lack the sense to make him happy. Anything and everything is, in fact, her fault.

Should you remind his mother that Harry had coughs or indigestion before he was married and while he lived under the maternal roof, you will receive the frozen reply, "Well, that's different."

Now, if your son has taken a wife unto himself and thereby endows you with the role of mother-in-law:—

Don't make up your mind from the start that he is going to be unhappy.

Don't tell his wife what, in your opinion, is the only way to take care of his happiness and his safety.

Don't look at him steadfastly, when he has been married a short while, and then turn round to his wife and tell her he is getting thin.

Don't ask him dramatically if he feels ill or what is on his mind.

Don't sit at his table and tell his wife not to give him this or that to eat.

Don't try to make him feel dissatisfied with life.

Don't tell him, in front of his wife, about all the other wives you know who have turned out failures.

Don't, if his wife is pretty, tell other people that she is a "doll."

If you want the young couple to have a happy time, the surest way of playing your part successfully is for you to make a fuss of

the young wife. Show her that you like her; tell her that you would have dreaded handing over your son to many of the girls he knew, but you had no such fears in her case. Make her like you; if she likes you she will see to it that her husband does not neglect you. And, if you do all this, your daughter-in-law will be happy; your son will be happy and they will both strive to make you happy.

IX

THE GRANDCHILDREN

MOTHERS-IN-LAW have curious notions about grandchildren. Of course, there are some who worship their children's children and look upon them as angels of perfection, even when a totally different description would be nearer the mark.

Nevertheless, there are many, and they are very numerous, who seem to think that their grandchildren will never grow up properly unless they interfere. And so, they interfere.

Now, by interfering, the mothers-in-law immediately make themselves unpopular and cause trouble all round.

It is ten to one that if the parents cannot

bring up their children properly there is very little that the mother-in-law can say or do which will have any effect. Accordingly, their interference is wasted, in any case.

Of course, we know that the mother-in-law once took a hand at bringing up children, otherwise she would never have risen to the dignity of a mother-in-law. But she should realise that all that was a long time ago; that things change rapidly; that children have changed; that she has changed, and that any views she may have on the upbringing of children are next door to worthless.

A generation ago, parents demanded that their youngsters should approach them with a sort of Victorian servitude. To-day, they want no more than to be viewed as equals or pals. Now, the average mother-in-law knows nothing of all that, and when sonny talks to his dad as he would a brother, she is scandalised and utters some remark about, "If I had ever spoken to my father in that way . . ." and so on. Of course, the whole point is that what would have happened in her day does not matter one iota in these days.

Not only that, but what does dad think about his mother-in-law's remarks? He looks upon them as not so much a criticism of the child as of him and his wife. And, not unnaturally, he fumes inwardly and wishes the dear lady would mind her own business.

Probably he says nothing at the time, but waits until his mother-in-law has gone and then ventures to make some pertinent remark to his wife. The wife is thus thrust between two fires. She remembers her mother before she was a mother-in-law and has a natural loyalty to her. At the same time, she knows her husband is right, since she holds exactly similar views to his. Nevertheless, she does not admit that much, as it is *her* mother who is concerned. We all know how the affair will end. It will end in a row between husband and wife—two perfectly harmless and worthy creatures. And while the row is reaching its climax the mother-in-law will be comfortably wending her way home.

A friend told us recently that her mother-in-law had spent the previous week-end with her and that she was exhausted by the time the mother-in-law departed. Her chief cause for complaint was respecting the way the mother-in-law had criticised the little grandchild, aged five.

Here are some of the criticisms which the mother-in-law expressed:

"Why don't you make Betty clear her plate? You should never let her get down from the table until she has."

"It is a pity you let Betty put her elbows on the table. When she grows up and has to wear evening dress she will have ugly elbows."

"If I were you, my dear, I would stop Betty sniffing. It's such an unpleasant habit to get into, and bad habits are so hard to get out of."

"I should never let Betty talk to you like that. And, of course, I notice she never says *Please*."

"Betty is very disobedient; I called her just now and she never came."

"Why don't you make Betty more tidy? She is quite old enough now to keep her hands clean. If she does not start to take a pride in herself now, she never will."

"Don't let Betty eat such a lot of sweets. I'm sure it's not good for her. You know they spoil her teeth." (In parenthesis, the sweets, it should be added, were given to Betty by grandma, and the remark was made when the child was eating her first one.)

"You know, Betty has exactly the same look in her eyes as your brother has." (The child's uncle is not noted for good looks.)

"Don't you think Betty ought to be able to read a little by now?"

"I wonder who Betty takes after when she walks like that."

"I don't think I've heard Betty say *Thank you* once."

Could there be any wonder that Betty's mother was overjoyed when her mother-in-law's visit came to an end?

X

LIVING WITH YOUR MOTHER-IN-LAW

IT often happens, through deaths in the family or other unfortunate circumstances, that a time comes when a mother-in-law reaches the stage of having no home of her own.

The children, presumably, are all married and living their own lives, perhaps in various parts of the country. The question then arises as to what is to happen to the bereaved lady.

All sorts of projects will be considered and, then, one of the daughters may graciously offer her mother a home with her.

Naturally, the daughter is to be commended for her action though, of course, she does not wish for any praise from us. She argues to herself that her mother is in an unpleasant position and that the trouble has come at a time when she is getting on in years and needs looking after.

Let us say quite bluntly, the project is fraught with dangers.

It is difficult to give the reasons why the mother-in-law *cum* daughter or son-in-law *ménage* can end so unfortunately, because there are so many different ways to spoil the peace of the home, but here are a few:—

(a) Mother-in-law wants the children to keep quiet while she is having her sleep, and she wants to sleep most of the day.

(b) Mother-in-law thinks her son-in-law gets more of the wife's attention than she does and is jealous in consequence.

(c) Son-in-law thinks just the reverse, and is jealous in consequence.

(d) Mother-in-law gradually strives to rule the home according to her notions and the son-in-law puts his foot down.

(e) Mother-in-law sets out to teach the children how to behave and becomes unpopular all round.

(f) Mother-in-law makes her daughter into a slave, and the son-in-law holds his peace for a while, but eventually there is the inevitable outburst.

(g) Mother-in-law tries to set her daughter against the husband, with varying degree of success.

(h) Every member of the family is too preoccupied with business or pleasure to make a fuss of the mother-in-law and she speaks her mind plainly.

Such are the things, some of them unimportant at the outset, which cause friction in a dual *ménage* of this kind. Ask any couple who have tried it; they will tell you that they embarked on the " joint forces" with every intention of making the arrangement a success; but within three months they knew they had been foolish, and within six months they were hoping for some way out of their purgatory.

Of course, all that is said here about a mother-in-law living with her married children applies equally to the married children living with their mother-in-law.

XI

FOOD FOR THOUGHT

HERE are some real tabloid tragedies which can be read as cautionary tales.

(A. C.—Cardiff.)—My mother-in-law did not lose much time in showing what she was made of. My wife and I planned to get married on a certain day, but the day did not suit my wife's mother. To please her, I got a day off from the office and we had the ceremony a fortnight earlier. As these arrangements made it necessary for me to turn up at the office on the following day, I stipulated that the wedding should be a quiet one. My mother-in-law agreed, and all those "in the know" were sworn to secrecy.

Everything went swimmingly on the appointed day and not a soul at the office had even an inkling. Next day, I turned up at the office as though nothing had happened. Loud cheers greeted my entry and copies of *The Daily* —— were thrust under my nose. There, in the "Weddings" column, were all the facts. My mother-in-law had sent the information to the paper.

(W. B.—Surbiton.)—Can you beat this? We planned to go to a tiny place in Devonshire for our honeymoon. We arrived late on a Saturday night, and on the following Monday afternoon were dumbfounded to see my husband's mother walking along the only street in the place. "I thought I would give you a nice surprise," she said, as she rushed up to us. It was a surprise, right enough, and for the rest of the time she followed us wherever we went, until at last we made a practice of getting up at 6 a.m. and going out of the place, not returning until nightfall.

(F. G.—Essex.)—Believe it or not, it is true,

nevertheless. We had been married two years and my mother-in-law was staying with us. I happened to walk into the dining-room and was just in time to see my mother-in-law give my wife a resounding smack on the face. I was taken aback, and in the heat of the moment gave the said lady a piece of my mind. I don't know even to-day what the trouble was all about; but this I do know—my wife refused to speak to me for more than a week because I had been rude to her mother! And, until then, we had never had so much as a quarrel.

(P. B.—Guildford.)—My wife's people are not noted for good looks and I often wonder why fate was so marvellously generous to her. Soon after our baby was born, my mother-in-law turned up to see the little darling. She was enthusiastic about its charms, as she had every cause to be. Gazing on the little creature she hazarded the remark, "I wonder whom it takes after?" And for two hours she was minutely discussing "the points" of all the members, near and far, of my wife's side of the family.

At last she decided that it was the "dead spit" (horrid remark) of my wife's Uncle Fred. Not once did she speak of anybody on my side of the family. Was that done purposely or did she not know any better?

(S. P.—Bedford.)—My mother-in-law drops in four or five times a week. She usually comes in during the afternoon and stays to dinner. When I arrive home, she is there chatting with my wife. She gives me a nod and goes on talking. Talking, I may say, is her strong point. I have to sit down and get on with my meal, and hold my tongue. If my wife turns to me and tries to ask me something, my mother-in-law butts in with, "But listen to this," or "The best of it all was . . ." You cannot silence her, do what you will. We would be out when she arrived were it not that the youngsters have to be considered. Naturally, they anchor us to the spot, we have to grin and bear it.

(M. F.—Liverpool.)—My husband's mother is the limit. Whenever she comes, which is often, she gazes at my husband and says how thin and ill he is looking. She asks if there is anything the matter, and then looks round at me as though she thinks I am starving him or poisoning him. As a matter of fact, Jim is as fit as a fiddle and is, I believe, putting on weight. The dear lady only says these things as a part of a campaign to make Jim dissatisfied with his married life. If I were to tell her, one day, what I think of her, I imagine it would give her the chance she wants. She would turn round instantly and tell me I was killing her poor, dear boy.

(C. S.—Harrow.)—My mother-in-law is always pleading poverty; also, she is always remarking on the new clothes I have. I don't think I have more or even as many as most girls in my station in life. The upshot of it all is that Bert is everlastingly giving money to his mother. She squanders it on theatres, holidays, clothes, and so on. What he gives her enables her to have things and do things which we cannot afford. Is it right that we are compelled to go without in order that she may be extravagant? I do think it speaks well for Bert, as it shows he is generous and thoughtful, but how do you imagine I feel when his mother comes home from a tour in Italy and asks me why I don't go, it's so lovely there. And all the time I know Bert footed her bill!

XII

THE WEDDING PLANS

THOUGH it may seem like putting the horse after the cart, we have purposely left this chapter to take its place near the close of the book. This is because it is a non-recurring part of a mother-in-law's duties.

We will suppose that a son or daughter has intimated to the family circle that he or she has definitely decided to be married on a certain date. The question is, *What does the mother do?*

In the case of the son's mother, the position is easily stated. She has really nothing to do except, perhaps, to send a friendly, not formal, note to the son's future wife or his future mother-in-law, whichever seems preferable, stating how pleased she is at the prospects of the union. Of course, she may not be pleased, but a letter to this effect will do more good than harm and it is advisable to write it.

In the case of the daughter's mother, things are very different. She has a number of duties to perform. The first is to call the two young people together and discuss the necessary plans with them. If the mother has acted reasonably during the courting days, this meeting need be no more than a friendly chat; but if she has adopted a high-handed attitude towards the young man, it will be a rather strained affair.

Anyway, the chief points to discuss are:—

(a) The style that the wedding is to take and (b) who are to be the guests. Of course, "style" translated into ordinary words largely means "cost" and the cost devolves by nature on the mother and father of the girl. As they have to meet the bill, it is only common sense that they should have the largest share in saying how the occasion is to be conducted; but beyond that the parents must be passive. What the mother must understand is that it is not her wedding, and she must not expect to have her own way. If, suppose, the young couple prefer a quiet wedding, it is not for her to stand out for something that will stagger the whole neighbourhood. She has definitely to bow to the wishes of those really concerned.

Next, as to the invitations. The usual plan is for two lists to be drawn up; one to include the girl's friends and relations, the other those of the man. As far as possible, the two lists should be of the same length; but in practice it generally happens that the girl's list is the longer.

The girl's mother has no sort of veto on the names figuring on the man's list. She must accept the names, and if there are any that cause her displeasure, there is only one thing for her to do, and that is to grin and bear it. It is certainly not the time for her to show pettiness. She may not be enamoured

with the young man's parents and she may
hate his sisters and aunts; but if they are on
the list, there they will have to remain. It is
not infrequent for the mother to put all her
own family's relations on the list and then
to begrudge the man a meagre handful of
invitations. Of course, all that is putting the
daughter in an invidious position and giving
her a bad start.

The ceremony can take one of many forms; but the only form that calls for any comment is the Church ceremony. Briefly, the first consideration is to be punctual, and for the whole congregation to be gathered before the bride arrives with her father. Thus, the two mothers have no part at all to play; accordingly they go direct to their seats. The girl's mother will sit in the front row of pews on the left of the church and the man's mother in the front row on the right.

When the ceremony is over, the two mothers should repair to the vestry, along with other close relatives and friends of the bride and bridegroom, and it is usual for them to sign the register. There is no compunction on them to do this; but, if one does, the other should do so also.

After the ceremony come the festivities, and it is here that many a tragedy has been enacted. Often, the occasion is the first real meeting of "his people" and "her people," but probably the two have expressed their opinions of the other side of the family many times before. Whatever the opinions, and whether one side has all money and no culture, whilst the other has all culture and no money, the differences ought to be sunk for the occasion and a spirit of tolerance should prevail.

In many cases, a report will be sent to the local paper. Usually, the information for this is supplied by the bride's parents, who should furnish the matter within a few hours of the event. Anyone who has to deal with these reports consistently, as we have to, will know that it is the bride's mother who supplies the information as a rule. And these reports can be monuments of pettiness in their original form. In a number of cases they have to be toned down and amended before they can be printed. The unsavoury practice in question is to set out the names and qualifications of the bride's relations at long length and to dismiss those of the bridegroom in an insignificant manner. It is just one way that some mothers-in-law have of giving their side of the family an importance which they are not prepared to grant to the other side.

Naturally the time comes—after the honeymoon, probably—when the bridegroom reads the report. He discovers that his is a family of no importance, but that his wife is the great-great-granddaughter of Mrs. So and so. He is not impressed; but he knows exactly where to bestow his thanks. He waits his time and, later on, his mother-in-law wonders why he is so cold to her.

XIII

THE RIGHT SORT OF MOTHER-IN-LAW

WHILE everybody is conscious of the fact that some mothers-in-law are remarkably unreasonable, no one will deny that there are many mothers-in-law who are perfectly charming and delightful.

Perhaps you who are reading these lines are a mother-in-law with a heart of gold. If that is so, it would almost be impertinence on our part to offer you our congratulations. We do, however, hope that your son or daughter-in-law recognises his or her good fortune and extends to you a suitable measure of gratitude.

But perhaps you are about to become a mother-in-law or have only recently assumed the important role of being one, and are anxious to perform the duties with tact and generosity. Then, may we offer you some words of good counsel.

Try to welcome the newcomer properly. Make him or her feel a part of the family. Don't treat him or her as a visitor, but as someone more to you than a visitor.

It will not lower your dignity, but will add very much to it, if you set to work to find out the trivial likes and dislikes of this new relation of yours. And when you have discovered them you should pander to them. Here is a case in point. Suppose the person in question is coming to your place to dinner, this evening, and you have found that he or she has a liking for a certain dish. Provide this particular fare and drop a hint, not blatantly of course, that it has been served because you believe he or she likes it. The said person will feel honoured and will unconsciously make a mental note that you are a good sort. Little acts of this kind can be multiplied indefinitely and they all help. Of course, your own child will be highly delighted if you display a measure of affection for the one he or she has married. And, instead of the marriage drawing your own child away from you, it will open up new and fresh bonds of affection. That is where your reward will come in. More than likely your position will be much better established than that of the young couple. Money, for instance, will mean more to them than to you, since they have recently spent considerably on getting the new home together. There must be many small things they sorely lack and which you can afford. If you use your detective instincts and secretly find out what these things are, think what nice little surprises you can give them!

Above all, treat the newcomer every bit as affectionately as you do your own child. For instance, do not remember the birthday of your child and forget all about the other one's. If you do, it has the effect of making the other one feel out of it; whereas, if you remember his or her birthday, it helps magically to draw the ties of affection much closer.

Of course, you will never take sides. If it so happened that your own daughter came to you and, in a fit of weakness, grumbled about her husband, there is no reason why you should not be sympathetic, but at the same time your best plan is to try to laugh the troubles away and to point out that every rose has its thorn. If you take up the cudgels and tell your daughter that her husband is this and that, she may agree with you at the moment, but, when the dispute has blown over, your remarks will ring in her ears and she will hate you for them.

Thus, by showing a friendly interest in the welfare of the young couple and letting them see that you are the right kind of mother-in-law, you not only afford them considerable pleasure, but you can earn their gratitude and gain comforts and satisfaction for yourself.

XIV

We have now come to the end of the story, and if you have not already done so you will set down this book and pass judgment on what we have written.

Before you do so, we would like you to recall the very first statement we made. It was to the effect that there are two main types of mothers-in-law, i.e., those you would never suspect as holding this particular office and those who leave no doubt about it in your mind.

Presuming that you are a mother-in-law, you will no doubt ask yourself into which group you would be rightly placed. Having decided the point and found yourself a member of the former class, we believe you will applaud our straightfoward denouncement of the latter class. In fact, you will be indignant with such people for the way they bring opprobrium on what should be a very honourable and lovable relationship.

If, however, you find yourself relegated to the latter class, it is more than likely that you will be none too pleased with our arguments. If we might be allowed to make a suggestion, it is as follows: You have been pilloried and are angry. In a day or so, you will be able to think over all we have said dispassionately. Your anger will have, at any rate, lessened. Then, and not before, ask yourself if certain of our strictures do not apply to you. The only truthful answer will be "Yes." Well, that being so, turn over the leaf and start again. It's never too late to mend.